DIGGING UP THE PAST

ÖTZI THE ICEMAN

BY TRUDY BECKER

WWW.APEXEDITIONS.COM

Copyright © 2026 by Apex Editions, Mendota Heights, MN 55120. All rights reserved. No part of this book may be reproduced or utilized in any form or by any means without written permission from the publisher.

Apex is distributed by North Star Editions:
sales@northstareditions.com | 888-417-0195

Produced for Apex by Red Line Editorial.

Photographs ©: Andrea Sabbadini/Alamy, cover; Paul Hanny/South Tyrol Museum of Archaeology, 1, 6–7, 8–9; iStockphoto, 4–5; A. Ochsenreiter/South Tyrol Museum of Archaeology, 10–11; Eurac/Samadelli/Staschitz/South Tyrol Museum of Archaeology, 12; Leopold Nekula/Sygma/Getty Images, 14, 18, 19, 24; Klaus-Dietmar Gabbert/dpa-Zentralbild/picture-alliance/Newscom, 15, 16–17; H. Wisthaler/South Tyrol Museum of Archaeology, 20, 22–23, 29; Shutterstock Images, 25; Gianni Giansanti/Gamma-Rapho/Getty Images, 26; Natacha Pisarenko/AP Images, 27

Library of Congress Control Number: 2025930918

ISBN
979-8-89250-534-5 (hardcover)
979-8-89250-570-3 (paperback)
979-8-89250-640-3 (ebook pdf)
979-8-89250-606-9 (hosted ebook)

Printed in the United States of America
Mankato, MN
082025

NOTE TO PARENTS AND EDUCATORS

Apex books are designed to build literacy skills in striving readers. Exciting, high-interest content attracts and holds readers' attention. The text is carefully leveled to allow students to achieve success quickly. Additional features, such as bolded glossary words for difficult terms, help build comprehension.

TABLE OF CONTENTS

CHAPTER 1
ICY SECRET 4

CHAPTER 2
UNDER THE ICE 10

CHAPTER 3
OTZI'S BODY 16

CHAPTER 4
LIFE LONG AGO 22

COMPREHENSION QUESTIONS • 28
GLOSSARY • 30
TO LEARN MORE • 31
ABOUT THE AUTHOR • 31
INDEX • 32

CHAPTER 1

ICY SECRET

In September 1991, two people hike through the Alps. They make their way across the snowy land. Suddenly, they spot a dark shape on the ground.

The Alps are a mountain range in Europe. They run through several countries.

The hikers crouch down to look closer. A body is sticking out of the snow. The hikers call for help. The police come.

FAST FACT

Hikers found the body in the Ötztal Alps. So, the man became known as Ötzi.

When hikers found the body, snow near its head and shoulders had melted.

People found several weapons and tools near the body. These items were also buried in ice and snow.

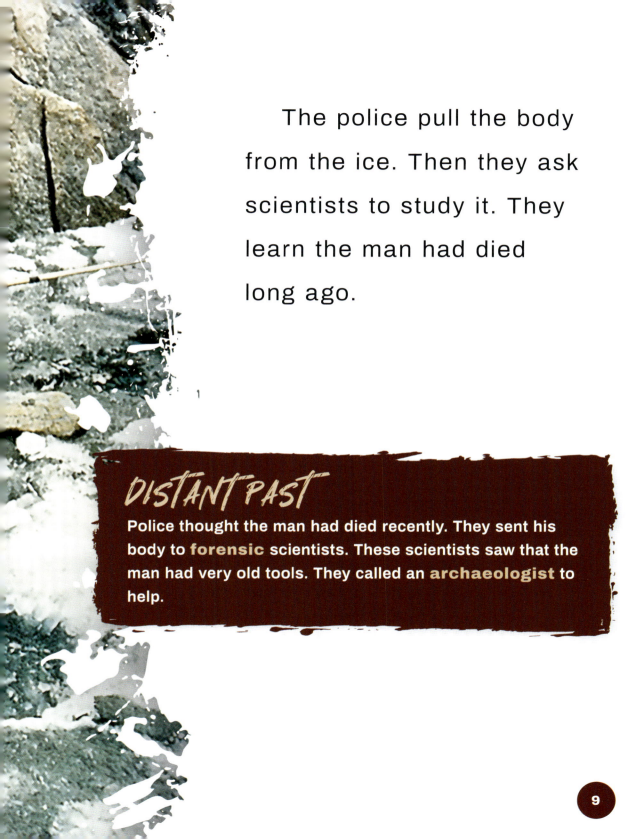

The police pull the body from the ice. Then they ask scientists to study it. They learn the man had died long ago.

DISTANT PAST

Police thought the man had died recently. They sent his body to **forensic** scientists. These scientists saw that the man had very old tools. They called an **archaeologist** to help.

CHAPTER 2

UNDER THE ICE

Ötzi the Iceman was an ancient man. Hikers found his body in the Tisenjoch pass. That is near the border of Italy and Austria.

Scientists created models of what they thought Ötzi looked like.

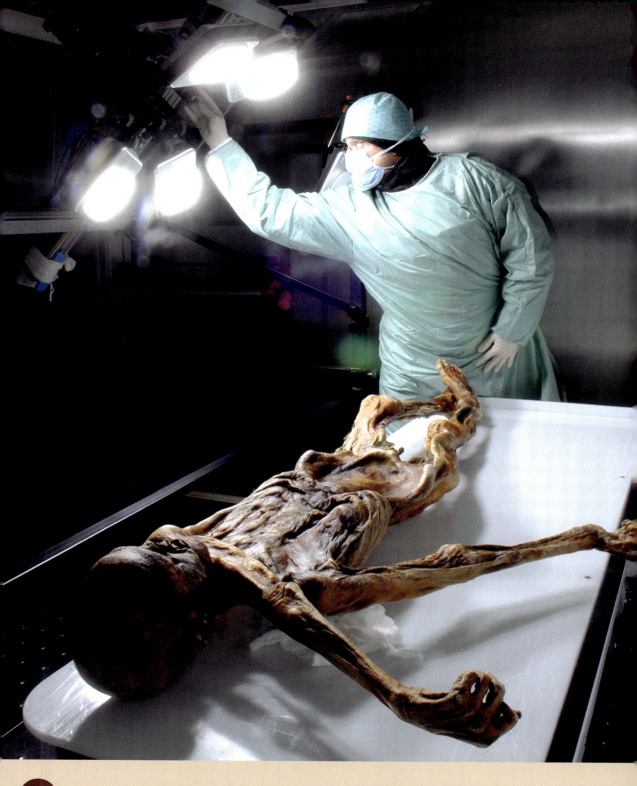

Ötzi was buried by a **glacier**. Ice kept his body cold. That preserved it. His skin and **organs** stayed **intact** for thousands of years.

FAST FACT
Bodies preserved in ice are known as "wet mummies."

◀ Often, soft body parts rot. But Ötzi's skin, brain, and muscles were intact when he was found.

Ötzi's shoes had grass stuffed in them. This would have kept his feet warm.

Much of Ötzi's clothing was preserved, too. He wore a coat of animal skin and fur. He had a belt, cap, and leggings. And he wore shoes made from animal skin.

ÖTZI'S ITEMS

People found a backpack near Ötzi. They discovered an axe and a dagger, too. They also found a bow and arrows. And a bark box held coals for starting fires.

Ötzi's backpack had a wood frame. This replica shows how it may have looked.

CHAPTER 3

Ötzi's Body

Scientists studied Ötzi's bones. They learned he died at about 45 years old. They also found an arrowhead in his shoulder. That wound may be why he died.

Scientists found the arrowhead inside Ötzi in 2001. They created this replica of it.

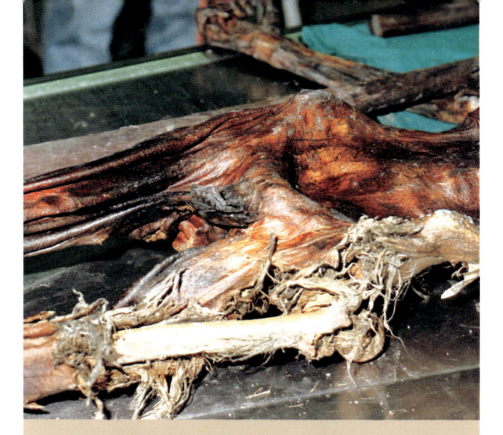

Police accidentally damaged the body when taking it out of ice. One officer ripped parts of the leg.

However, scientists are not sure. Ötzi had several broken ribs. His hand had a bad cut. Scientists also found signs that he had been sick.

ÖTZI'S LOOKS

Ötzi was about 5 feet 2 inches (157 cm) tall. He had dark hair and a beard. And he had 61 tattoos. These ink marks are all over his body.

Ötzi's tattoos look like black lines or crosses.

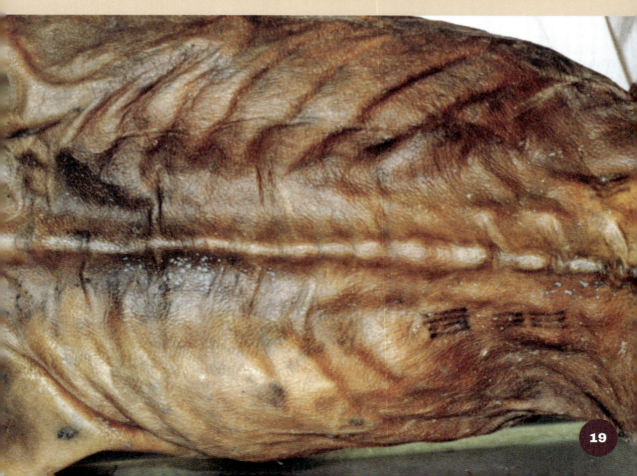

Scientists also used **carbon dating**. They learned that Ötzi lived about 5,300 years ago. This was during a time called the Copper Age.

FAST FACT
Ötzi is the oldest known wet mummy in the world.

◀ People found a copper axe near Ötzi's body. This tool helped scientists guess when he lived.

CHAPTER 4

LIFE LONG AGO

Studying Ötzi helped scientists learn about Copper Age life. Some of Ötzi's **injuries** were old. They had healed. So, scientists think he may have fought often.

Scientists found other people's blood on Ötzi's dagger.

By looking at Ötzi's teeth, scientists could tell what kind of water he drank. They learned where he grew up.

Scientists also studied what was in Ötzi's stomach. They found meat and grains. He likely lived among people who hunted and farmed.

FAST FACT
Ötzi likely traveled before he died. His stomach held plants from high and low in the mountains.

Ötzi's last meal included wheat and deer meat.

Ötzi is kept in the South Tyrol Museum of Archaeology in Bolzano, Italy.

Today, Ötzi and his items are in a museum in Italy. The museum built a freezer to hold him. It stays very cold. Visitors can see Ötzi through the glass.

OTHER MUMMIES

Scientists have found wet mummies on other mountains. But **climate change** is causing glaciers to melt. Some bodies may stop being preserved.

In 1999, scientists found frozen mummies in Argentina. The bodies are more than 500 years old.

COMPREHENSION QUESTIONS

Write your answers on a separate piece of paper.

1. Write a few sentences describing what people learned by studying Ötzi's body.

2. Would you want to visit Ötzi in a museum? Why or why not?

3. About how many years ago did Ötzi live?
    - **A.** 61
    - **B.** 1,991
    - **C.** 5,300

4. How would the contents of Ötzi's stomach help show that he traveled?
    - **A.** The food he ate came from different places.
    - **B.** The food he ate all came from one place.
    - **C.** He didn't have any food left in his stomach.

5. What does **crouch** mean in this book?

*The hikers **crouch** down to look closer. A body is sticking out of the snow.*

    A. dig through a mountain
    B. jump up into the air
    C. bend down toward the ground

6. What does **preserved** mean in this book?

*Ice kept his body cold. That **preserved** it. His skin and organs stayed intact for thousands of years.*

    A. kept something unharmed
    B. broke something into pieces
    C. made something very warm

Answer key on page 32.

GLOSSARY

archaeologist
A person who studies long-ago times, often by digging up things from the past.

carbon dating
Calculating the age of something based on the amount of a certain carbon in it.

climate change
A dangerous long-term change in Earth's temperature and weather patterns.

forensic
Using science to help solve crimes.

glacier
A large, slow-moving body of ice.

injuries
Types of harm to someone's body.

intact
Unharmed or whole.

organs
Parts of the body that do certain jobs.

BOOKS

Carlson-Berne, Emma. *Mummies Around the World*. Lerner Publications, 2024.

Markovics, Joyce. *Ice Mummies*. Cherry Lake Publishing, 2021.

Murray, Julie. *Ötzi the Iceman*. Abdo Publishing, 2022.

ONLINE RESOURCES

Visit **www.apexeditions.com** to find links and resources related to this title.

ABOUT THE AUTHOR

Trudy Becker lives in Minneapolis, Minnesota. She likes exploring new places and loves anything involving books.

INDEX

A
Alps, 4, 6
archaeologist, 9
Austria, 10

C
carbon dating, 21
clothing, 14
Copper Age, 21, 22

F
food, 24–25
forensic scientists, 9

G
glaciers, 13, 27

I
Italy, 10, 26

O
Ötztal Alps, 6

T
Tisenjoch pass, 10

W
wet mummies, 13, 21, 27

ANSWER KEY:
1. Answers will vary; 2. Answers will vary; 3. C; 4. A; 5. C; 6. A